Know You
You Beautiful
Badass

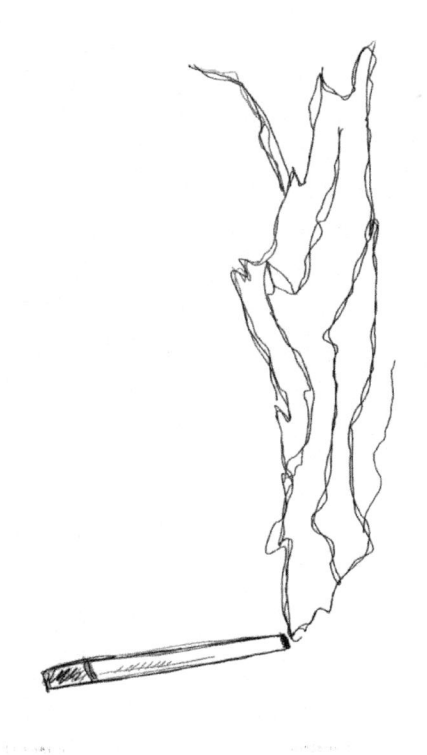

Calah Olson

Copyright © 2012 Calah Olson

Written and Illustrated by Calah Olson.

@Calaholson

All rights reserved.

ISBN: 9798646620904

DEDICATED TO:
J & A

My siblings, my best friends, and my biggest inspirations.

CONTENTS

	Acknowledgments	i
1	Thoughts	1
2	Overthinking/Fear	6
3	Give Yourself a Damn Break	11
4	What Really is Self-Love?	16
5	Who are You?	21
6	Passions	25
7	Let Go	29
	Quotes/Inspiration	31
	About the Author	35

Hello! Welcome to our book. I say "ours" because you and I are going to go on a little journey together. This journey is going to show us how to better love ourselves and recognize our personal power. Now listen, I'm no fancy writer; I really wouldn't even consider myself as someone who is good at writing. But this book is about you and your growth, not about me and my terrible grammar skills and mouth of a sailor. This book is a compilation of some very important lessons that I've learned in my short life so far. I've always struggled with my self-worth/self-love but I eventually learned to accept who I am and love the life I live. I think there are a few things in this book that will show you how to do the same. I hope you enjoy this little journey that we are about to go on together, and I hope that by the end of this you will finally see how fucking awesome you really are. Think of me as your friend/guide through this whole book. I'll be your "tour guide" to help you find the power that resides in you.

ACKNOWLEDGMENTS

Thank you to Chloe Bleu Nuttall, Katerina Backstrom, Jonathan Crampton, and Samantha Untalan for being wonderful examples of self-love and their unshakable enthusiasm for growth. You inspire me every day.

1 THOUGHTS

Studies have estimated that the mind thinks around 60,000-80,000 thoughts each day. That's about 2,500-3,300 thoughts per hour! So pretty much all we do all day is create thoughts whether we recognize them or not. We spend the majority of our lives purely thinking. Take a second and just ask yourself what percentages of your thoughts are negative? If we are really honest with ourselves, our thoughts are most likely negative 50% or more of the time. When you really think about it, isn't that kind of sad? That we have this amazing capability to create ideas that shape the world around us, yet we waste 50% of it solely on negativity???

So why are we this way? Why are we consistently having thoughts that break us down instead of lift us up? I'll tell you exactly why. We have literally been programmed to do so. From birth we are taught to judge everything and everyone around us. We were taught that judgement is the way to see if someone or something is "safe" or "good" for us and our societies. Our parents taught us how to act, who not to talk to, what to wear, how to present ourselves, and what success is. We were literally conditioned to think a certain way so that we would not stick out in society. We were wired to be submissive, colorless, numb beings when in reality, we are meant to be unique and colorful.

We were trained by society to judge people by their outer exterior to the fullest extent without even recognizing we are doing so. Think about it. Have you ever judged someone walking down the street because of their looks? Have you ever thought someone was "ugly" because of what they were wearing? We all honestly have. But here's the thing, you didn't actually think that person was ugly; you were taught by society that they were unattractive. The most beautiful person in the entire universe can go completely unrecognized due to the fucked up labels society has written all over them. Society loves labels.

It's not really your fault for being stuck in this way of thinking and the habit of labeling/judging others. It is all you've ever known and you can't really change something you are unaware about. Once you recognize it you can break it. Now that you are aware of it, let's change it. This way of living and labeling is unhealthy not just for others but also toxic to your self-worth.

Not only are you judging everyone around you without knowing, you're also doing that to yourself. When we scrutinize and judge ourselves down to the bone, we lose a lot of self-love and self-respect. We start to believe that we are worthless, unimportant, and that we will never be "good enough." I think it is time to break this way of thinking and this habit of heavily judging yourself. It may sound difficult but you can literally re-train your mind to think in a more positive and self-loving way.

Re-training your mind by using very simple techniques can change your life more than you think.

It has been said that it takes 21 days to create a new habit and it takes 90 days to create a lifestyle. A lot of people call this the 21/90 rule. What I'm saying is that it doesn't take eternity to change your habit of negative thinking. It can literally only take you 21 days. If you are ready lets break it...

So before we create the new habit of thinking more positively and in a self-loving way, we have to break the old habit of thinking negatively. You have to tear down the wall before you can plant the garden. The one thing that helped me learn to block out the negative thoughts is what I like to call the "Cancel Alert." The Cancel Alert is used by literally saying the word "CANCEL" in your head whenever a shitty negative thought comes to mind.

> CANCEL!
> Stop the negative thought!
> Replace it with positivity!

It may sound like the dumbest thing but it actually works. Let's say you're standing in the mirror and you have a thought that says "I'm ugly." Immediately after you have that thought use your Cancel Alert. Scream Cancel in your head if you need to! Then after you've said "cancel," think 3 positive thoughts about the subject you were just judging. In this case it was about your appearance. So then say 3 things that you do love and enjoy about yourself.

By using the "Cancel Alert" you are now training yourself to shut down negative ways of thinking. The more you do it the easier it gets and the more results you will see. It's just like trying to do the splits. You're not going to get the splits the first time you stretch, but if you stretch everyday it will eventually become easier and easier until finally you're in your damn splits!! Try it right now. Maybe you had a negative thought about yourself today. Go back and remember what that thought was.

Write it down here.

Now write 3 things that are positive to counteract.

_____
_____
_____

Keep it Positive

It definitely can be hard at first but you'll get the hang of it! I promise. For the next 21 days work on using the "Cancel Alert" as often as you can and watch how your way of thinking shifts. It will soon become second nature and your mind will thank you for it!

Positive mind   Positive life

"Start each day with a positive thought and a grateful heart."
— Roy T. Bennett, The Light in the Heart

Know Your Worth You Beautiful Badass

Don't Overthink Everything You Do.

2 OVERTHINKING/FEAR

Overthinking is something we all just love to do. It's pretty much the seed of all your worries and anxieties. When we overthink, we take one thought and basically make it snowball effect by adding more and more thoughts. Then eventually that thought disappears into the snowball of your overthinking. Most of the time, our overthinking tends to be mostly negative. Let's say you were invited to a party your initial thought is, "Oh fun I'm excited to go and have a good time." But then you start to over analyze this party. You start to think,"Oh shit what if I'm too dressed up." "What if so-and-so is there?", "What if I'm awkward when meeting these new people and then they don't like me?", "What if something goes wrong?"

Now since you've allowed yourself to snowball you've created this assumption in your head that this party is going to be a shit show and not at all enjoyable. Overthink it can cost us a lot of amazing experiences in this life. It can cause you to become fearful about literally anything and prevent you from taking a hold of the beautiful opportunities this universe is going to bring you. Overthinking creates fear and who the hell wants to live a life of fear? No one! After all, if you are constantly in fear you aren't living life at all.

thought ⟿ [tangled scribble]

Overthinking and fear play hand-in-hand. You overthink because you're scared and you're now scared because you over thought. It's basically this never ending cycle that prevents us to live life to its absolute fullest. It also prevents us from being our true selves.

Overthinking = Fear
Fear = Overthinking

Have you ever found yourself scared to be raw? To express yourself truly and freely? Well that's all due to your overthinking/fear of yourself my friend; we overthink ourselves because we are scared of judgment.

Of course a little bit of HEALTHY self-reflection and self-judgment can help us improve and get rid of bad habits, but it becomes unhealthy when we judge every single minuscule aspect of ourselves including the things we enjoy. The world can be a very cold and an excepting place at times but that doesn't mean it's OK to be that way to yourself. You are a radiant being that is alive on this planet right here right now for a reason! You are **you** for a reason! Why hide that? If people don't except you for you then oh well! Not everyone's going to like you and not everyone's going to love you and that's OK. The only thing that matters is that you love yourself. A way to show yourself a little bit more love is to stop Overthinking everything you do. Stop overthinking what people think about you. **Stop being scared of yourself!**

There are little things that you can do throughout your day to help stop overthinking yourself. Example, when you're picking out an outfit in the morning stop asking yourself if this outfit is trendy or if other people will like it. If you like it and you feel confident in it, Then wear the fucking outfit!!! Self-expression is key to self-love so express yourself dammit! Don't be so quick to judge yourself.

Don't be so quick to be your worst critic. You've heard the saying "You are your worst critic," right? It's entirely true. We are the quickest to judge ourselves. We recognize our own flaws more than anybody ever will. Sometimes we tend to hyper fixate on them, thus making us only think about our flaws and ruining our self-image.
One thing that is helped me learn to not judge myself so quickly is this analogy:

[If you wouldn't say it to your best friend don't say it to yourself?]

This meaning if you wouldn't judge your best friend that harshly, why are you doing that to yourself?

To help get rid of this overthinking habit try doing one thing that pushes your boundaries every day. Do something that you usually wouldn't do because of the judgment of other people. Do something that you genuinely want to do, not something that you're doing to please someone else. Maybe it's wearing bright green pants, or wearing different make up, or coloring your hair a different color, whatever it is do it because **you** want to do it. Don't hold yourself back because you're scared of what other people might think. Start learning to not give a fuck.

Reminder: Fear = overthinking
Overthinking = Fear
Don't be so scared of yourself. Don't be so quick to judge yourself. Draw yourself doing something you are scared of doing because of peoples judgment

Don't be this guy……..

Know Your Worth You Beautiful Badass

3 GIVE YOURSELF A DAMN BREAK

Life can sometimes seem as if it will never slow down. One event after another; issues after issues that we are all frantically running around trying to fix. I can feel as though you don't have a single second to yourself. But here's the thing, life will never slow down for you, you have to command to. You have to take action into your own hands to take care of yourself and your mental state. You have to realize that you are in control; you are in the driver seat! Life is just a vehicle. When you feel yourself getting overwhelmed or overworked you need to step on the brakes. You need to give yourself a moment to breathe and relax. If you don't ever give yourself breaks you will eventually feel yourself beginning to suffocate.

[Sketch of a car labeled "LIFE" with "you" as driver; caption: "you are driving you are in control"]

We all need to recognize that we're all just tiny little humans, not robots that are created to work themselves into oblivion.

The stress of our daily lives can get in the way of our path to self-love. Sometimes we worry way too much about absolutely dumb shit that we forget to take care of our sanity! Sometimes our minds can feel like the junk drawer you have in your home. Full of tangled headphones, tangled power cords, and other random shit you don't know what to do with. You need to take care of yourself and your mind so you won't always be a pair of tangled up Apple headphones. You need to start allowing yourself to take a break, to disconnect from chaos for just a moment and take care of your needs. Because at the end of the day, all we have is ourselves. So why not treat yourself right.

[Sketch of tangled headphones labeled "Tangled Mind"]

Taking a break doesn't mean just taking your 15 minutes at your job, it means that literally taking a second to yourself anytime you feel you need it. Taking little breaks here and there helps us release all of that overwhelm so doesn't bottle up and destroy us. If you leave the water boiling too long soon it will overflow right? Think about it, it's actually easier to take small breaks here and there to help keep ourselves collected rather than having to pick up a million pieces after we explode.

Just taking a small break can help re-center you and collect your thoughts and emotions especially during a stressful time. It will also help you control your reactions and your thoughts. Taking a small break to reflect and unwind your tangled mind can help you see life in a new light.

If you need a break take a damn break!! Whether it's a walk out in nature or just treating yourself to a cup of coffee, you deserve the break. Life is supposed to be lived not merely endured so go take a minute to help your mind relax. A break can even be taking a few seconds to yourself to be mindful and grateful for where you're at. It can be a small quick meditation to remember that you need to appreciate the life that you're living. What defines a "break" will be different for everybody, it's personal and unique to what you and your soul needs.

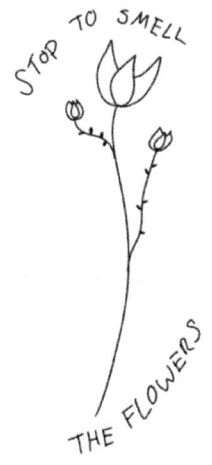

Do some self-reflecting today and find what it is you need when you take your break. What is it that re-centers and grounds you? Once you find that thing, write it down and remember to use it as often as you need to!

Life will be so dark if you never take a moment to stop and soak up the sun.

Be nice to yourself, give yourself a break. We both know you deserve one.

GO GIVE YO SELF A DAMN BREAK!

"The purpose of life is to live it, to taste experience to the utmost, to reach out eagerly and without fear for newer and richer experience."
— Eleanor Roosevelt

Know Your Worth You Beautiful Badass

4 WHAT REALLY IS SELF-LOVE?

Self-love. What an overused and watered down phrase. Today you may see hundreds of Instagram posts of people wearing a face mask with the caption #selflove. Or people blowing ridiculous amounts of money on material items and calling it an act of self-love. Maybe these things to make you feel good, great! There's absolutely nothing wrong with doing nice things for yourself but sometimes we need to understand that self-love is not fulfilled by just materialistic desires. Self-love starts on the inside. Self-love helps heal your soul and spirit.

Be nice to your soul.

Wikipedia defined self-love as, "regard for one's own well-being and happiness." meaning taking care of your own needs and not sacrificing your happiness and stability for others. Self-love basically means never settling for less than what you deserve.

Why is self-love so important?

1. Self-love helps you choose what is best in life for you.
2. Creates a healthy relationship between you and your own view/self-image
3. Hope you recognize your worth as a human on this planet. Self-love is an action you take consistently over time; it is not just a state of being.

Yourself.

Self-love can be many things it can be:
- Saying no to something you don't want to do
- Reading helpful books that help your growth
- Taking yourself out on a personal little date

- Being mindful of your gifts and talents
- Setting healthy boundaries
- Self-forgiveness
- Understanding your human and spiritual needs and providing for them

As I stated in the previous chapter about taking breaks, that can also be a form of self-love. Just like the breaks, your ways of self-love are also personal and unique!

Showing yourself some love can be very challenging when you do not recognize your beauty and worth. Your evil little inner monologue can tell you that you don't "deserve" self-love because you are "imperfect" or "too flawed." I'm here to tell you to shut that shit down.

You are worthy and valuable beyond comprehension. You are alive right now on this time on this planet for reason. Remember that you have a higher purpose than you know. You are a part of something big and something great. Your life and journey on this planet is not a mistake. You are a spiritual, divine, energetic being having a human experience. You are not just a human having a spiritual experience.

Write down 5 things that you personally can do to practice self-love!
1.
2.
3.
4.
5.

Reminder: Give love, get love.

"Dare to love yourself
as if you were a rainbow
with gold at both ends."
— Author-Poet Aberjhani

Know Your Worth You Beautiful Badass

5 WHO ARE YOU?

Who are you when no one is watching? I think the most important step in learning how to love yourself and learning how to harness your personal power is really getting to know yourself. Ask yourself this one question, do you really truly know who you are?

We all can get to really know ourselves by asking what truly fuels us in this life. What are you so passionate about that you feel it in every bone in your body? What is the spark that lights the flame in your heart to keep going? And I'm not asking you what is "cool" to like, or what your friends like, or what you were taught to like. I'm asking what **you** truly enjoy.

I am a firm believer that passion is the center/root of your life. Your passions affect who you are, how you act, and what you do.

Passion is the key.

If you are wondering and searching for what it is that you truly love and are passionate about, I think it's time you spent a little alone time with yourself to answer that question. When we are truly alone, that is when we are our most authentic part of ourselves. With no noise, no judgment of others, and no distractions, we can let ourselves just be.

Who are you when you're alone?

Taking time alone is a very important part of taking care of ourselves. If you don't already, I challenge you to take at least 30 minutes of your day to be alone and just hang out with yourself. By doing this, you'll be able to have a one-on-one conversation with yourself and steadily figure out who the hell you are!

Know Your Worth You Beautiful Badass

We can become so codependent sometimes. We are dependent on the thoughts of society in the thoughts of our peers that we forget we are our own independent soul with independent thoughts and interests. A key to finding who you are is allowing yourself to be independent.

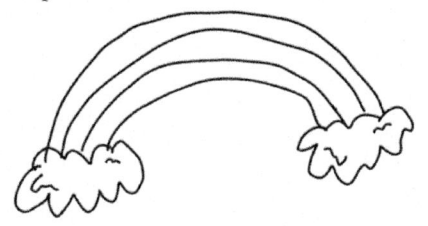

Be sure to allow yourself some alone time today to really get to know who you are and what you love. If you already know who you are and what you love then great! Still take some time to be alone and remember the things you love and why you love them! Remember and reflect on your undying passion for the things you enjoy.

Sit alone with yourself for at least 30 min a day and do some soul searching.

Write down 3 things you know you enjoy.

1.
2.
3

"To be yourself in a world that is constantly trying to make you something else is the greatest accomplishment."
— Ralph Waldo Emerson

Know Your Worth You Beautiful Badass

6 PASSION

As I stated in the previous chapter, Passion is a huge aspect of our lives and our personalities. It is such a huge deal that I decided I wanted to go a little bit more in depth with you in this chapter. Passion is defined as, "a strong and barely controllable emotion." A passion is something that you love with every ounce of your being. It is something you would cease to exist without. I believe that passion is the most important driving factor in everyone's life. Without passion we would have nothing. Without passion van Gogh would have never painted, Mozart would have never played, and Shakespeare would have never written. The most beautiful and invigorating things on this planet and in history are all rooted in passion.

I asked you in the previous chapter if you knew who you were and if you knew what you were passionate about. So what is it? What is something you would die without doing? You can literally be anything. No matter how weird or small. Passion is still passion.

If you don't know what you're passionate about yet that is OK. You will find it. It will come to you. Everyone is born with a passion and a purpose you do have one!

When you are trying to discover your true passion, reflect on moments in your life that you've truly felt fulfilled. It could be a time you helped someone, a time you performed, created, and even a time you spoke. It can be anything. The cool thing about us humans is that no two of us are exactly the same. We all have our own unique passions that fuel us. We are all built to think, act, and create differently.

Your passion is the secret ingredient to a life of happiness and fulfillment.

Whatever your passion is, let it consume you. Let passion in your driver seat. If you live your life through passion, you will never feel empty. Passion fuels the soul, while thoughts control the mind. Let your thoughts intertwine with your passion. With everything you do remember passion.

Just imagine what the world would be like without passion. The greatest works of art, literature, architecture, and inventions would cease to exist. Recognize that you are just like Van Gogh, Mozart, and Chopin. You have the capability to craft your own beautiful life through your passion just as they did. By living through your passion you will be living the way your soul is meant to.

"Let passion possess you and life will be as the heavens."

Know Your Worth You Beautiful Badass

7 LET GO

Letting go. Letting go of our past or our current unfulfilling life can be difficult. Learning to break the chains that we have been held down by for so long is the most important part of growth yet also the most beautiful. You have lived and thought a certain way up until this very moment in time.

It's time to grow my dear.

Take all your hurt, all of your negative ways of thinking, and all of your old and unfulfilling ways of life and put them in a box. Now take that box into an open field and set it on fucking fire. Those old ways do not serve you anymore. They are only holding you back and it's time for you to move forward. With every chapter we've read together I hope that this book has opened your eyes and to see how special you truly are. You deserve to show yourself love and that you are powerful beyond your own comprehension. You have a purpose. You are the writer of your own narrative, and it's time to start creating the fulfilling and loving life that you deserve.

I hope that something in this book even if it's only one sentence has helped you even in the smallest bit.

Thank you for sticking with me and going on this adventure together. Thank you for learning and growing with me in this book.

Thank you for being you.

Know your worth you beautiful badass.

You are worth it.
Sincerely,
Your new friend,
Calah

QUOTES/INSPIRATION

"Life is too short to waste any amount of time on wondering what other people think about you. In the first place, if they had better things going on in their lives, they wouldn't have the time to sit around and talk about you. What's important to me is not others' opinions of me, but what's important to me is my opinion of myself."
— C. JoyBell C.

"A person learns how to love himself through the simple acts of loving and being loved by someone else."
—Haruki Murakami

"Love yourself first and everything else falls into line. You really have to love yourself to get anything done in this world."
— Lucille Ball

"When you adopt the viewpoint that there is nothing that exists that is not part of you, that there is no one who exists who is not part of you, that any judgment you make is self-judgment, that any criticism you level is self-criticism, you will wisely extend to yourself an unconditional love that will be the light of the world."
— Harry Palmer

"To fall in love with yourself is the first secret to happiness."
— Robert Morley

"Don't you ever let a soul in the world tell you that you can't be exactly who you are."
— Lady Gaga

"Wanting to be someone else is a waste of who you are"
— Kurt Cobain

"Sleep my little baby-oh
Sleep until you waken
When you wake you'll see the world
If I'm not mistaken...

Kiss a lover
Dance a measure,
Find your name
And buried treasure...

Face your life
Its pain,
Its pleasure,
Leave no path untaken."
— Neil Gaiman, The Graveyard Book

Know Your Worth You Beautiful Badass

You are not small.

You are not unworthy.

You are not insignificant.

The universe wove you from a constellation,

just so atom, every fibre in you comes from

a different star.

Together, you are bound by stardust, altogether

spectacularly created by the energy of the

universe itself.

And that, my darling,

is the poetry of physics,

the poetry of you.

—Nikita Gill

ABOUT THE AUTHOR

Calah Olson is a young female entrepreneur who loves to challenge and question the rules of society. After her own battle with abuse, self-harm, and suicide, she decided to go on a journey to find healing and self-love.
Her intention with this writing is to promote self-love and encourage self-expression.

Know Your Worth You Beautiful Badass

Printed in Great Britain
by Amazon